animal planet™

I Am Machli
🐾 Queen of the Tigers 🐾
Level 2

Written by Brenda Scott Royce

Silver Dolphin

P1 PRE-LEVEL 1: ASPIRING READERS

1 LEVEL 1: EARLY READERS

2 LEVEL 2: DEVELOPING READERS

- Simple factual texts with mostly familiar themes and content
- Concepts in text are supported by images
- Includes glossary to reinforce reading comprehension
- Repetition of basic sentence structure with variation of placement of subjects, verbs, and adjectives
- Introduction to new phonic structures
- Integration of contractions, possessives, compound sentences, and some three-syllable words
- Mostly easy vocabulary familiar to kindergarteners and first-graders

3 LEVEL 3: ENGAGED READERS

4 LEVEL 4: FLUENT READERS

Silver Dolphin Books
An imprint of Printers Row Publishing Group
A division of Readerlink Distribution Services, LLC
9717 Pacific Heights Blvd, San Diego, CA 92121
www.silverdolphinbooks.com

ISBN: 978-1-64517-954-2
Manufactured, printed, and assembled in Shaoguan, China.
First printing, October 2021. SL/10/21
25 24 23 22 21 1 2 3 4 5

Hello! My name is Machli.
I am a Bengal tiger.

People call me the Queen of
Ranthambore.

Ranthambore is a national park in India. It is my home.

India

Here, I walk among ancient ruins. These palaces and forts were abandoned long ago.

This land was once ruled by kings. Now, it is ruled by tigers. And I am the leader.

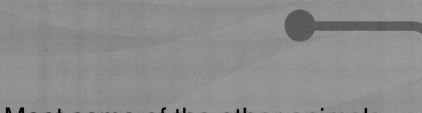

Meet some of the other animals that share this **habitat**.

There are monkeys, deer, vultures, and many other **species**.

Adult tigers each have their own **territory** that they defend.

As the strongest tiger in the park, I have the best territory.
It stretches for hundreds of miles!

This lake is one of my favorite spots. On hot days, I like to soak in the cool water.

Did you know that tigers are great swimmers? It's true!

Afternoons are for resting. Like all cats, tigers sleep a lot.
I doze up to fifteen hours a day.

At night, it is time to hunt. Tigers can see very well in the dark.

I am a **predator**, which means I must hunt to survive. Wild pigs and deer are some of the **prey** I hunt.

Tigers are built for hunting. We have sharp claws and long **canine teeth**.

Our powerful bodies help us run fast.

We have excellent hearing, too. Our large ears can rotate toward sounds. This helps us locate prey.

I hear something rustling in the grass. The hunt is on!

My stripes help **camouflage** me among trees and tall grasses.

I approach slowly and silently. Then I **ambush** my prey.

The hunt was a success.
Now I have food for my cubs.

Tiger cubs grow quickly, and they need lots of food to keep growing big and strong.

Tigers are mostly **solitary**, but cubs stay with their mothers for about two years.

Here I am with my fourth **litter** of cubs!

When they get older, my cubs will come with me so they learn how to hunt, too.

Cubs also learn to hunt through play. They chase, pounce, wrestle, and roll around. They practice skills they'll need as adults.

In play fights, no one gets hurt!

Real fights, though, are a part of every adult tiger's life.

Sometimes we battle for food.

Sometimes we clash over territory.

I always fight to protect my cubs, even when my **opponent** is bigger than me.

One day, my cubs were drinking at the lake.

Suddenly, I heard a crocodile's tail splash against the water. Its jaws snapped loudly as it tried to attack!

I quickly moved my cubs away from the water's edge. Then I gave the crocodile a warning growl. It didn't back down. So, I leaped onto its back.

The crocodile was twice my size, but it was no match for me!

The story of my bravery spread across the world. People come from far away to see me.

They take pictures of me and the other tigers that live here.

They have even made movies about me.

Do I look like a movie star to you?

I didn't mind the attention, because it is good for tigers if more people know and care about us. There are fewer than 4,000 tigers left in the wild. We are **endangered**.

Ranthambore is a **reserve**, which means its land is protected. The park rangers who work there are always looking out for us. Scientists are studying tigers to learn the best way to protect us, too.

Today, the number of tigers in India is growing!

All my cubs are grown up now. I don't run as fast or leap as high as I once could. I have scars from many years of battles.

I am getting older.

One of my daughters will now take over my territory.

When she has cubs of her own, she'll teach them to be strong and brave, just like I taught her.

I will move to a smaller territory knowing I raised a strong leader to take my place. I have done my job and am as proud as any mother could be!

Discovery

PROJECT**CAT**

CONSERVING ACRES FOR TIGERS

Discovery and others have a plan to help protect tigers where they live in the wild. It's a program called Project C.A.T.

Project C.A.T. is working to save and protect nearly one million acres of tiger habitat in India and Bhutan.

The goal is to provide a healthy habitat where tigers can thrive and their numbers in the wild can grow. Project C.A.T. hopes that its efforts will allow the number of tigers in the wild to double!

Saving habitat for tigers will also help other animals that share the land, such as rhinos, elephants, and leopards.

Glossary

ambush: to sneak up on and attack

camouflage: to blend in with the surroundings

canine teeth: fang-like teeth used to bite and tear food

endangered: at risk of disappearing from the Earth

habitat: the place where an animal lives

litter: a group of baby animals born at the same time

opponent: someone you defend yourself against

predator: an animal who hunts another animal for food

prey: an animal that is hunted by other animals for food

reserve: a place where the land and the plants and animals that live there are protected

solitary: living alone

species: a group of living things different from all other groups

territory: an area that an animal controls and defends